COMPLETE. PRICE ONE PENNY

SPIRITUALISM
EXPOSED,
Showing its origin, Immoral tendency, folly wickedness, &c.

LIGHTING UP A DARK SEANCE.

CONTENTS:

AN EXPOSE OF MODERN SPIRITISM.

"Spiritism and Spiritualism" are two totally distinct things. The latter means that truly Spiritual mindedness and steady pursuit of eternal life, which is beyond all praise, The former refers to that deadly error of seeking after familiar Spirits and striving to hold intercourse with the dead. Spiritualism is of and from God—Spiritism is of and from a totally different source. This distinction has been commonly overlooked, and in consequence, a most intelligent body of Christians ; the Swedenborgians have been called Spiritists, when the fact is, according to their publications, that they are utterly opposed to Spiritism. We think it truly right to mention this, as we have no wish to continue in a mis-apprehension, which has been cleared up to our mind. Swedenborg died 75 years before Spiritism commenced and in his works he predicts its coming, and warns his readers strongly against its horrible character.

THE ORIGIN OF SPIRITISM.

THE "Spirit" manifestations which have been so largely developed by rapping, table turnings, musical performances, &c., commenced in April, 1848, in the family of a person named Fox, who lived in a small wooden house at Hydesville, in the Town of Arcadia, Wayne County, New York States, U.S.A. The desire to hold converse with the invisible world was at that time greatly stimulat d by the celebrated Lectures and "Revelations" of a certain Andrew Jackson Davis, a young shoemaker of Poughkeepsee, U.S.A., given while Mesmerized by a Mr. Levingston, a tailor, and by a Dr. Lyon. The tendency of Davis's writings is in the direction of Universalism and Fourierism, and it is remarkable that while Dr. Lyon was a Fourierist, another most intimate associate of Davis, a certain clergyman named Fishbough was a Universalist, so that Davis's so-called Revelations were as much derived from the brains of his mesmeric friends as from any ultra " Spiritual" source. It will be seen that modern Spiritism originated simply in some out-of-the-w y Mesmeric performances, and so closely interwoven is Clairvoyancy with Spiritism that many persons have thought the one synonymous with the other. But this is only partially true ; while every Spirit medium must we believe be a Clairvoyant su' ject, there is yet a wide

Distinction between Mesmerism and Spiritism.

Mesmerism is a purely natural phenomenon, and is simply the control of a passive mind by the will power of an active mind, expressed by means of the natural magnetic influence with which every human being is more or less endowed. The operations of Mesmerism are confined to this world; both the operator and the subject are living in the body. There are however many feats of Spiritism which cannot be adequately explained by the Mesmeric theory alone, although not one of their genuine performances can we understand be executed except by the aid of Mesmeric action in one way or another. According to the Spiritists own statements, Mesmerism is the Magnetisation of a human subject by a living being, and Spiritualism is a similar Magnetisation by a Spirit. Asked for an explanation of this, a Spirit medium is reported to have said :—

"Suppose I magnetise you to-day, and that I, the mesmerist, "speak, write, act, through you—you being unconscious—that is "Mesmerism. Suppose, further, that I die to-night, and to-morrow, "I, a Spirit, come and magnetise you, and then speak, and write, and "act through you—this is Spiritualism." Now arises the question,

"What is a Spirit?"

We have no sympathy with the notion that a Spirit is some vapoury shadowy thing, without substance, form, or power. The best authority, the Bible, teaches that "there is a *Spiritual body*" as well as "a natural body," and it is very likely that this "Spiritual body" is the soul which lives in the outer world after the body is dead. At any rate, if man does live after death in a Spiritual body, in a spiritual world, and all Christians believe this, then a Spirit must be a human being having substance, form and power. Those who wish to examine the subject will do well to purchase a little work, entitled :— "The Nature of Spirit," by Rev. C. Giles, price 6d., and sold at the Swedenborgian Repository, Bloomsbury Street, London.

How Mediums are Controlled by "Spirits."

At a certain Seance held in Boston, in 1868, a "Spirit" was asked to explain the "*modus operandi*" of the mediumistic control, and the reply is said to be as follows :—

"As a Spirit *who by nature has no right to the medium's body*, my "first step is to come and hold communion with the Spirit who owns "the body. I ask that Spirit, 'will you yield me up the control of "your mortal form for a short time?' The answer is, generally, 'I "will.'"

Here are some important admissions, viz: that intercourse with Spirits is not according to nature, and that no one gives himself up to the diabolical influence except willingly—the Spirits, powerful as they are, *cannot* control an unwilling medium ; and although we have heard of some exceedingly annoying tricks they have played upon converted Spiritists, those who *keep their minds unbiassed* are perfectly safe. What man of sane condition, morally and mentally, would allow either his body or his mind to be a theatre into which some restless and possibly disreputable ghost may mutter some gibberish, toss guitars about, drain the nervous power and suck the brains (often too scanty) of the gulled " medium." ? We read further, " The Spirit (of the man) is subject to the entire control of the predominating Spirit— it is in a word magnetised by the Spirit—*held in perfect subjection*, and asleep as far as external life is concerned." The mode in which the Spirit thus obtains possession of a Medium is strikingly analogous to the mode in which vice :

> " That monster of so fierce a mien,
> That to be hated needs only to be seen,"

controls its votaries ; submitting itself at first, with plausible questionings and seeming propriety, and then when consent is given, taking entire possession of mind, soul and body to the utter destruction of all. How many Spiritists have fallen victims to such arrant folly and wickedness it is impossible to say. Further on will be found a few instances given as warnings to would-be " Investigators." The following testimony shows clearly that

SPIRITS ARE OF FULL OF DECEIT AND TRICKERY :—

Mr. A. E. Newton, formerly Editor of the *Spiritual Age*, says, " It is alleged to be possible and common for Spirits of a certain class " to *assume the appearance of other Spirits*, or of other persons still in " the body *so completely*, that the disguise *cannot be detected by ordinary* " *sight seers.*"

This may be so, and *hence the common evidences of the identity of Spirits are little to be relied on.* And again,

" When two persons are closely in sympathetic or magnetic " *rapport* with each other, the *images* that are in one mind may be " perceived as *objective realities* by the other."

The operator forms an image of some person or object in his own mind, which the subject (if well under control) instantly sees the same thing or person as an objective reality.

So " positive Spirits " around the persons in a seance " may " present the image of any person with whom they are familiar, and " it may appear as a reality to the impressible medium."

Another noted Spiritualist, Andrew Jackson Davis, formerly Editor of the *Herald of Progress*, says :—

" A wise " (? cunning) " and strong-minded person in the Spirit " world has the power to make visible to the eyes of mortals, the " exact appearance or resemblance of the body it wore before death, " and this * * * to the minutest particular, even to the repro-

" duction of the appearance of the habiliments, &c., by which the
" person was identified while a resident of the earth.   *   *   All
" intelligent spirits are great artists ; they can easily represent them-
" selves as being old or young, as in worldly dress or flowing robes, as
" is deemed best suited."   What more is needed to show that no value
whatever attaches to the utterances and acts of these vagrant Spirits
through their mediums ?

Another Spirit Medium says :—

" The correctness of communications from Spirits, depends upon
" the more or less perfect mesmeric control the spirit has over the
" medium ? "   *   *   *   " The power of the spirit to control the
" medium's mind is *stronger* than that of a good mesmerizer."   *   *
" The Spirits control by means of the magnetic aura or animal
" magnetism."   In cases of " entire physical control " the power of
the Spirit " *pervades the entire physical body* " as well as the mind.

Here we have a series of astounding admissions most damaging to
the cause of Spiritualism.   We learn that the spirits operate just as a
mesmeriser does, that the whole affair is a very much a matter of
imagination, and that no reliance whatever can be placed upon the
so-called messages from departed friends, about which so much fuss is
made.   Everything said, done, or shewn at the Seance is an imposture,
since the medium is operated upon, not by good, but by foolhardy and
carnal-minded Spirits, who are only too pleased to have the opportunity
of disobeying God's laws, by breaking through the wholesome regula-
tions he has made against the intercourse with the dead.   Surely we
have quite sufficient of hell upon earth already, without seeking to
open up in the persons of " mediums " avenues of approach for the
very lowest fiends of hell into the houses and hearts of mankind.

How nice to be kicked out of one's earthly tabernacle, that a Spirit
of questionable antecedents may play havoc with our moral furniture ?
So much wrong is possible and has actually been accomplished to
females and others by Mesmerism, that every pure, sound, healthy
mind recoils from the idea of submitting itself, soul and body, into the
entire control of some human being of stronger will and more developed magnetic influence, but probably not very high moral character.
Not that every Mesmerist is necessarily bad, but the practice is
susceptible of such grave mis-direction, that some precautions should
always be exercised in meddling with so dangerous a subject.   But if
Mesmerism—performed very frequently with great medical benefit—is
in unskilful or malevolent hands, productive of so much mischief ;
how much more that Spiritual Mesmerism, whereby the mind is
controlled by some spirit, of whose antecedents character proclivities,
nothing can be known and who has moreover the power of
concealing for a time its real character.   The Mesmeric operator is
amenable to law, and to a certain extent he is (if he be a professional
man) known but this is not the case with " Spirits.'   What wonder
that Spiritism has turned out to be one of the vilest plagues that ever

harassed human life : oftentimes however so carefully cloaked under religious guise, that detection of its real character is not easy.

Admitting this intercourse with " Spirits " to be a fact, it is one of the most infernal, deceptive, and mis-leading pursuits, that it is possible to conceive of. It makes one regret that the English language possesses no phraseology sufficiently powerful to adequately stigmatize the arrant folly and wickedness of this Spiritism. We have now before us a mass of alleged Spirit communications which are nothing less than BLASPHEMOUS ; some brief extracts of the milder sorts of which we will quote and the reader will see that the pretensions of Spiritism are very good to look at.

They say, e.g.—" The doctrines of Christ are to be re-established " (we did not know they had been dis-established) " in their purity by Spiritualism, which embraces all that tends to elevate man !" It will " inaugurate the Millennial era ; " " exert a reformatory power among the nations ; " it will " absorb all denominations of Christians ;" It " stands upon the same foundation as Christy ; "—It embraces all the virtues and strikes at the root of all evils, social, political, and religious ; " It is " the Gospel of the present age ; "—" the best news that ever came to earth ! "

Now let us compare these utterances with the evidence published by Spiritists themselves, and we shall get a glimpse of the

FEARFUL IMMORALITIES CHARGED AGAINST SPIRITISM BY CONVERTED MEDIUMS.

The following extracts speak for themselves, our space precludes full quotation. We would only say that no witnesses are considered so credible, as those who have practically undergone the experience of which they speak.

Extract from a Sermon by Dr. P. B. RANDOLPH, (a celebrated Spiritist Lecturer) preached in Clinton Hall some years ago, and published in the *New York Tribune.*

" For nearly ten years have I been seeking rest for my weary soul." * * Spiritualism, he says he now believes " to be the most tremendous enemy of God, morals and religion, that ever found foot-hold on the earth ;—the most seductive, hence, most dangerous form of sensualism that ever cursed a nation, age or people. * I was a medium about eight years ; have been in the trance state, 2500 times ; made 3000 speeches and travelled over several different countries. My health of mind and body was well nigh ruined. To-day I would rather have the *Cholera* in my house, than be a Spiritual medium." Dr. Randolph then goes on to describe his

ATTEMPTED SUICIDE BY DIRECTION OF SPIRITS.

" Once in a moment of despair, I, with dreadful intent, severed the blood vessels of both arms in four places. Chance led a man to approach me, ere the lamp of life had quite gone out, and by super-human exertions, I was saved." This attempted suicide, Dr. Randolph says :—" I charge to demonism and the infernal doctrines taught by many invisibles. The anti-Bible, anti-God, anti-Christ-Spiritualism is unrighteous, destructive, disorderly and irreligious. For seven years I held intercourse with what purported to be my mother's spirit. I am now firmly persuaded that it was nothing but an evil spirit and infernal demon, who in that guise, gained my soul's confidence, and led me to the very brink of ruin. FIVE of my friends DESTROYED THEMSELVES, and I ATTEMPTED it by DIRECT SPIRITUAL INFLUENCES. Every crime in the calendar has been committed by mortals moved by viewless beings. *Adultery, fornication, suicides, desertions, unjust divorces, prostitutions, abortions, insanity ! !* * * I charge all these to this scientific Spiritualism. It has banished peace from happy families. separated husbands and wives, and shattered the intellects of thousands. * It is subversive of human dignity and public morals ; it is destructive of all we hold most dear and cherish most sacredly. It robs us of faith in Christ, without giving us a substitute. It robs us of our refuge in religion, and cultivates th> intellect (?) at the expense of the heart." Elsewhere, Dr. Randolph says :—Spiritualism is a synonym for all falsities and lies, a cloak for all crimes, adultery, murder and lust, it weakens man's intellect and individuality, changes his worship of God, into a worship of Ghosts. I have a volume of over 60 closely written pages of names, of those who have been drawn down from respec ability, moralty, wealth and intelligence, to the filth of Free Love, to poverty and to insanity itself ! "

Mr. T. L. HARRIS, a noted high-class Spiritualist, who has published a number of " Celestial Revelations." of a very mystical description ; and who delivered a Lecture in London some time ago also testifies to

ADULTERY, THROUGH SPIRITISM.—WIFE DESERTION.

He says :—" The marriage vow imposes no obligations in the view of Spiritualism. Husbands who had for years been devotedly attached to their wives * * * have abandoned them and formed criminal connections with other females, because the spirits have told them that there was a greater Spiritual affinity between these husbands and certain other women, than between them and their lawful wives. Wives, too, the most devoted and loving, and true to their husbands, * * had left their husbands and children, and lived in open immorality with other men, *because the spirits had told them so to do.*"

We are accustomed to look upon Mormon Polygamy as a terrible crime, but does not this almost eclipse it in virulence ? "

THE " FREE LOVE " SCANDAL

is another of the fruits of this Upas Tree Spiritism.

Every one, almost, has heard of the Institution at Berlin Heights, Ohio, in which the principle of "free love," *alias* indiscriminate lust, is carried out. In one of their publications, marriage is denounced as " an odious monopoly of the opposite sex,"—" it ought to abolished," and men and women be " brought together by *passional attraction !"* Dr. A. G. Parker, Chairman of a Spiritualist " Social Relations " Committee, actually brought before the National Spiritual Convention, held at Chicago, in August, 1864, a resolution which declared that " the only true and natural marriage is an exclusive conjugal LOVE between one man and one woman,"—not be it observed a lasting union since the cessation of such " *exclusive* love " is quite enough to annul the marriage. Those who doubt the correctness of this construction should hear what Mrs. Julia Branch is reported to have said, when a similar resolution was discussed at Rutland. She described the institution of marriage, " as the sole cause of women's degradation and misery." " She must demand her freedom, *her right to have children, when she will and* BY WHOM. Another of these dear creatures ! a Mrs. Lewis is reported to have said, at Ravenna, Ohio :—" To confine her to love ONE man, was an abridgment of her rights. Although she had one husband in Cleveland, she considered herself married to the whole human race ! " (It is a pity the whole human race cannot get released from the unequal bargain.) " All men were her husbands, and she had an undying love (?) for them." Then she clinches the nail by this astounding statement :—

" What business is it to the world, whether one man is the father " of my children or ten men are ? I have a right to say who shall be " father of my offspring ! "

Certainly, Mrs. Lewis, though we do not see how you are to tell ! Another Spiritualist, who became the father of an illegitimate child by the direction of the Spirits ;—a Mr. J. Speere thus defends his conduct in the *Spiritual Telegraph*, of December 18, 1858 :—

" It is reserved, for this, our day, *under the inspiration of the spirit world,* for a quiet, equable, (?) retiring (?) woman, to use up in the dignity (?) of her womanhood, and declare in the face of her oppressors (!) and a scowling world ! *I will be free ! !* * * and no man or set of men, no church, no state shall withhold from me the realisation of that purest of all inspirations, (!) inherent in every true women *the right to re-beget myself, when and by whom, and under such circumstances, as to me seem fit and best.*"

THE TALE OF A DESERTED WIFE.

The following is a copy of a letter recently received from a poor, ill-used wife, which speaks for itself. It is dated from Jefferson, Ashtabula Co., Ohio, June 5, 1858, and the writer's name is Mrs. A. Hunter. " Mr. Editor, I saw an article in the *Ashtabula Telegraph*, a few days since * * giving an account of the rescue of a young and lovely woman, by her husband from the den of infamy at Berlin,

(Ohio.) * * * Let her thank a kind providence that she is restored to the arms of a loving and kind-hearted husband, and is not, as I am, a deserted and heart-stricken wife and mother. * * My husband was the founder of the Berlin Free Love Institution. A year ago or more he left home ostensibly on business, but he only roamed around in search of free love companions, having found a small number of which he took them to Berlin, and founded the infamous den of lust, which now exists there. He left me with three little children to provide for. I have stood for four days in the week, over the wash-tub, labouring until my strength has given way entirely, for the sake of a little money with which to feed my children."

Astonishing Revelations by an ex-Spiritist.

Mrs. Cora Hatch, is a noted Trance speaking Medium. Let us hear what a former husband of her's, (Dr. Hatch) who travelled extensively with her while she was giving Lectures on Spiritualism, says :—After stating that his long experience of Spiritualism entitles him to be heard, and that the fear of offending many Spiritualists could not deter him from warning the inexperienced against the dangers of Spiritualism ; he goes on to say *inter alia*. " I believe there is a powerful influx of *infernal* error into nearly all mediumistic minds * * I have heard much of the improvement in individuals, in consequence of a belief in Spiritualism—*with such I have no acquaintance.* But I *have* known many whose integrity of character and uprightness of purpose, rendered them worthy examples to all around, but who *on becoming mediums and giving up their individuality, also gave up every sense of honor and decency*" He then summarises some of the results of Spiritism. " Iniquities, which have justly received the condemnation of centuries, are openly upheld ; Vices which would destroy every wholesome regulation of society are crowned as virtues ; prostitution is believed to be fidelity to self ; marriage an outrage on freedom ; love evanescent and like the bee, should sip the sweets wherever found ; bastards are claimed to be spiritually begotten * * God is * * simply a permeating principle ; the Bible a libel on common sense ; and Christ a mere " medium ! " Further, after expressing his belief that these perfidious doctrines are rapidly increasing he says :—" The most damning iniquities are everywhere perpetrated in spiritual circles, a very small percentage of which ever come to public attention. * * It is worse than useless to talk to the Spiritualist against this condition of things, for those who occupy the highest position among them, are aiding and abetting in all classes of iniquites which prevail amongst them. Abrogation of marriage, bigamy, accompanied by robbery, theft, rapes, &c., are all chargeable to Spiritualism." He had for a long time been so excited by the spirit manifestations, that he paid little attention to the evils of them, but he says : " During the past eight months, I have devoted my attention" to a critical investigation of its moral, social and religious bearings and I stand appalled before the revelations of its awful and damning realities, and *would flee fom its influence as I would from miasma which would destroy both soul and body.* Spiritualism and prostitution, with a rejection of Christianity, are twin sisters, which everywhere go hand in hand." With but "little enquiry," he had counted "over 70 mediums, most of whom have wholly abandoned their conjugal relations, others living with their paramours called "affinities," others in promiscuous adultery, and still others who had exchanged partners. Old men and women who have passed the meridian of life, are not unfrequently the victims of this hallucination. Many of the mediums lose all sense of moral obligations, * * they are made to yield to the powers which for the time being control them."

Another authority is Mr. J. F. Whitney, who was Editor of the New York *Pathfinder*, and formerly a warm advocate of Spiritualism. He says :—that " after a long and constant watchfulness, seeing for months and years its progress and practical workings ; our honest conviction is that the manifestations through the rapping, tapping, writing and entranced mediums have a baneful influence ; create discord and confusion ; inculcate false ideas, approve of selfish individual acts, and endorse theories and principles,. which when carried out, DEBASE AND MAKE MEN LITTLE BETTER THAN THE BRUTES.

After pointing out from his experience that the " believers " in Spiritualism and " particularly mediums " progress (sic) from lives of morality to those of sensuality and immorality, that it " gradually and cautiously undermines the foundations of good principles : " in power-ful language he urges " those who are moving passively down these rushing rapids to destruction," to pause ere too late to " save them-selves from the blasting influence which those manifestations are causing."

Dr. Wm. Potter, another very experienced American Spiritist and a medium, author of a work entitled, " Spiritualism as it is," gives important testimony :—" Fifteen years of critical study of Spiritual literature, an extensive acquaintance with the leading Spiritualists, and a patient, systematic and thorough investigation of the manifestations for many years, enable us to speak from *actual knowledge* of Spiritualism, as it is. Spiritual Literature is full of the most insidious and seductive doctrines, calculated to undermine the very foundations of morality and virtue, and lead to the most un-bridled licentiousness. "We are told," says Dr. Potter, *inter alia*, "that man is a machine, and not to blame for his conduct ; sin is a lesser degree of righteousness ; those who act the worst will progress the fastest ; lying is right ; slavery is right ; murder is right ; adultery is right ; that sexual union is necessary for health and development, but that as persons develope, they become unadapted ; and *variety* is more productive of mental and physical development.

Hundreds of families have broken up, and many affectionate wives deserted by affinity seeking husbands. Many once devoted wives have been seduced and left their husbands and tender helpless children to follow some " higher attraction." Many well disposed, but simple-minded girls, have been led away by affinity hunters, to be deserted in a few months with blasted reputations ; or led to deeds still more dark and criminal, to hide their shame."

It is a notorious fact, that leading teachers, noted mediums and and popular speakers have deserted companions, obtained divorces, gone off with affinities, or practised promiscuous intercourse to get spiritual element, or to impart vital magnetism for the cure of disease. The outside world has no conception of the folly of True Love and licentiousness among Spiritualists, especially on the part of "healing " and developing mediums."

At the National Convention of Spiritualists, at Chicago, called to consider the question of a national organisation, the only plan approved by its Committee, especially provided that no charge should ever be entertained towards any member, and that any person without any regard to moral character, might become a member. Conventions of Spiritualists have accepted as delegates, and elected to office well-known persistent habitual libertines. The late National Convention of Spiritualists at Philadelphia, through its Committee, *refused* to read a proposition to dis-fellowship known libertines, but formed a permanent national organization with annual delegated Conventions, from which the lowest and most beastly licentiousness shall not exclude any one. Parting husbands and wives is one of the notorious tendencies of Spiritualism. The oldest and most influential teacher of Spiritualism has two wives' each, of whom he encouraged to get divorced, before he married them. We heard one of the most popular impressional speakers say to a large audience, that she was compelled by spirits to secede from a husband, with whom she was living very happily."

The following statement is made by a correspondent of the *Bible Echo* :—

" We are personally acquainted with one who claims to be *Christ's* medium, and a medium for the higher order of spirits, as the apostles and other holy men ; and yet we heard a prominent Spiritualist say, in a Concert Hall, Philadelphia, in October, 1875, that this very medium was a vile wretch, and that he held dark circles (séances) with persons in their nude state. The same medium has so abused two wives, that they cannot live with him. He says he is to have seven wives. In connection with all this we have rarely heard a man who would talk purer morals than this person. After hearing him speak of Jesus and the " Christ principle," one might suppose him to be a true follower of our Saviour, but when the test is applied, the whole is found to be only Satan's counterfeit."

Instead of Christianism being synonymous with Spiritualism, as claimed by the spirits and spiritualists, they are as unlike in their moral influence as Christ and Belial We might as well affirm that a house of ill fame was a nursery of virtue, as to say that Spiritualism exerts a good moral influence upon Society." To which we cordially say, hear! hear! But some may say "all your evidence is from America, how does that affect Englishmen?" America is the home of Spiritualism, there it exists in all its freedom and, hence its true character is most clearly represented. The reason why the same horrible practices do not (if they do not) occur in England, is because they would be at once put down with a strong hand. That England however is not entirely free from similar nefarious practices, is well known to those who are behind the scenes. A dear relative of the writer of this—a widow of prepossessing appearance—was not a very long time ago, waited upon by an affinity hunter, who by continual observation, had observed her residence and loneliness. She was naturally much terrified to hear that there was a "spiritual affinity" between her and her frowsy looking visitor, who left some spiritual papers and promised to call again. In the interim she was advised to inform the affinity, that a relative of hers, (a gentleman) was an enquirer into Spiritism, and would like to see a live spiritist. This message was duly delivered, but, from some cause, the affinity never returned to claim his other half. The dread of "lynch law" probably spoilt the "affinitation."

We will now give some specimens of

"SPIRITUAL AERONAUTS AND HIGH FLYERS."

Many of our readers will remember the famous and absurd story told about Mrs. Guppy, a medium who was reported to have been "conveyed instantaneously from within her breakfast parlour at Highbury, (where she was engaged making up her housekeeping accounts,) to a *locked* room at 61, Lambs Conduct Street, the residence of another notorious medium, where she was found in a state of trance or unconsciousness, *upon* a table, around which ten persons were engaged holding a seance."—Mrs. Guppy took her seat on the table it is gravely stated, "with her house-keeping book and pen in her hand, with the ink still liquid." Naturally, this astounding story created much surprise and amusement at the time; (June 3rd, 1871) but it seems to be out-done by the following tale of

"THE TRANSFERENCE OF A SCEPTIC FROM WITHIN A LOCKED ROOM TO A DISTANCE OF A MILE-AND-A-HALF."

The account appears in the "Medium and Daybreak," of Dec. 5th, 1873, a Spiritualist newspaper. It is headed by what is truly described as an "IMPORTANT NOTICE," stating that it had been "offered to the *Daily Telegraph, Standard* and the *Daily News*, but was refused by those journals," much to the credit of their respective editors.

Space forbids our quoting the report at length, but the following is a fair summary. The Seance was held on Nov. 2, 1873, at 9-50 p.m., in the house of Mrs. Guppy before mentioned, ten persons including Mrs. Guppy, and a certain sceptic whom we will call B were present

The door was, it is stated, locking inside, and the key left in it, the window shutters closed and fastened, and other means of excluding light resorted to. All being ready, the Seance commenced, and the sitters were told to make what requests they pleased of the Spirits. Mrs. Guppy's wish was "that somebody might be carried out of the room." Soon the table, a cumbrous one, began to rock so violently, that the circle was broken several times, and some of the sitters "lost their hold of each other's hands." Suddenly "B" was missed, and when a light was struck, was nowhere to be found. The Seance had then lasted about 20 minutes. The room was examined, but it is said that the doors, shutters, &c. were just as they had been left. The house and garden were searched, but no "B" was to be found, and his great coat and hat had also disappeared. The party were then "informed by the Spirits" that B had been carried off. Mr. B's account is then given, by which it appears, that after the rocking of the table, he lost consciousness and found himself next rolling off a stable roof into the back yard of a house about 1½ miles from Mrs. Guppy's house. After trying several doors, he obtained admittance into the house and found the family, who were "acquaintances of his" at supper, the time being about 10-5 p m. The report then attempts an explanation of this extraordinary tale :—

Mr. B, although a sceptic, was not "considered likely to have played his friends a joke," nor was it thought that one of the others had assisted him out of the room in the dark and locked the door after him. "Time" is admitted to be "of the essence of the matter," and it certainly does seem strange that Mr. B did his little aerial flight in considerably less than no time, since he is said to have left Highbury at 10-10 p.m., and arrived at Holloway at 10-5 p m. But let that pass, "clocks in private houses are not regulated with railway accuracy," and how could "we foresee that time would be an element of so much importance!" Surely the "Spirits" could have "foreseen" this and given the correct tip! The report then goes on to state :—

That "this event is not one of mere 'weight-carrying' but involves the passing of solid matter through solid matter, thus further complicating the case in favour of scepticism." But instead of explaining, they make matters worse, by narrating the following :—At two very remarkable seances held at Mrs. Guppy's house, one of the visitors asked for a sunflower, almost immediately a whole sunflower plant over six feet high was placed on the table together with half a bushel of mould about its roots. At another sitting some forty articles were brought, including (among fruit, flowers and vegetables,) two living gold fish, a live lobster and two live eels,—one of which to the no small alarm and annoyance of Mrs. Guppy was placed around her neck. The difference between bringing a sunflower plant into closed and bolted room, and taking out Mr. B—a gentleman of over fifteen stone weight—is little more than that of degree.

Anyone reading the above tale with his eyes open and uninfluenced by spirits of any sort, would imagine that Mr. B had it may be designedly—it may be in a state of confusion produced by Mesmerism—slipped out of the door, (which was locked after him,) taken a cab and started off to the first place that occurred to him. But it needs a very elastic imagination to stretch to the belief—ours would break in the effort—that Magnetism, Spiritism, or any other ism, can drag a 15 stone sceptic through a brick wall, without leaving a hole, a trace of sulphur, or even a singe on the wall paper behind;—plant him down stairs in the hall, put on his coat and hat, and hurry him off through the air on a clear moonlight night, at a time when the streets are full of idle people, drop him on top of a stable roof,—and all in five minutes under no time! If this is the sort of thing Spiritualism is to accomplish for us poor benighted mortals, we have an additional reason for wishing its devotees a speedy farewell. So little credence was attached to the foregoing narrative, that it soon died a natural death. The Editor of the "Medium," gullible as he seems to be, and anxious as he is to sell his paper, spoke upon it with bated breath and quickly dropped the subject. One of his observations, deserves re-production. He says:—"It is widely known in London that the gentleman in question is an eminent photographer. He has been heard to ridicule the manifestations, and that he would some time or other put a narrative into the mouths of Spiritualists which would bring their pretended experiments into contempt," which he has most successfully accomplished!

THE DARK SEANCES

Are a peculiar feature in modern Spiritism. It is said that the wave vibrations of light interfere with the actions of the Spirits. Is it not more likely that these Spirits "love darkness rather than light because their deeds are evil?" If Spiritism was true and good for man, it would never need to be shrouded in darkness, which serves two purposes, to conceal any trickery, and to plunge the mind into a state of nervousness. Our frontispiece illustrates the effect of a sudden lighting up of a Dark Seance, by means of a "bull's eye." The Medium is found on the floor of the platform, in the midst of his performances and his assistant makes a hasty escape. Something similar actually occurred at a Seance at Newcastle-on-Tyne, a short time ago, which was fully reported in the papers. It was said the sudden light caused the mediums suffering, but it seems more clear that their trouble arose from being discovered performing the Spirit manifestations themselves. At a Seance held at Belfast, during the recent visit of the British Association, a light was suddenly struck, and the medium hastily scrambled up from under the table, where he had been rapping on the floor.

The following account of the AWFUL DEATH OF A SPIRITIST Which occurred in December, 1878, is taken from the *Daily News*. No doubt the wide publicity given to the matter, contributed in no small degree to that decreasing interest in Spiritism, which is now so marked in certain quarters :—

BIRMINGHAM, Sunday Night. This evening, at the Athenæum Rooms, Temple-row, a spiritualistic service was being held, and in the course of it a medium named Benjamin Hawkes, a toy dealer of New street, in this town, addressed the meeting. He spoke for fully half an hour, appearing to be in his usual health, and then he described with startling vividity a seance in which the Apostle Peter had manifested himself to the assembled spiritists Peter had clasped hands with him, and he (Hawkes) felt the close pressure of the Apostle's grasp. From this he argued that it was quite possible to understand how Thomas of Didymus thrust his hand into the side of "the Personification of Divine Love." The instant these last words were out of the speaker's mouth he fell back on a chair behind him. There was great excitement, for the meeting believed Hawkes was under strong "spirit control." A few seconds elapsed, and a surgeon came up to the medium, and found him dead. The meeting broke up in wild confusion. Perhaps a more exciting scene never occurred than the death of this man, with the wild words of his fervent belief fresh on his lips.

The verdict on the poor fellow was "died by the visitation of God," a verdict which caused much perturbation in the breast of the worthy Editor of the "Medium." Our readers will hardly credit the statement, that in a number of this paper published shortly after Mr. Hawkes' demise, it was stated Mr. Hawkes' spirit presented itself and held intercourse with a certain professional medium only the day after this awful occurrence !

Here is an account of some WATCH ENGRAVING BY THE SPIRIT JOEY, said to have occurred at Westmoreland Hall, City Road, London :

"When the music ceased, the paper I was taking notes with was suddenly taken from my hand and whirled round the room, and returned in a few seconds with the following words written in pencil : "Joey wants you to report this." After many little things had been done, the spirits were asked if they could engrave names on the watches of any of the gentlemen present. Three watches were immediately extracted from the pockets of three gentlemen, and in less than two minutes one was returned to Mr. S, with the name "Joey" on it. Another was hung on the gas bracket, and the third was taken out of the room, the spirit remarking that he would take it to a vice and have it properly engraved, and return it on Sunday.

The watch was returned to me at Mrs. D's by Mr. E, he at the same time stating it had been found on the floor at Mrs. M's, Bethnal Green Road. The cases were engraved as follows :—" John Haxby " and " Charles Louis Napoleon Bonaparte, February 20, 1875."

How any one with a well-balanced mind can believe such absurd nonsense as the above, is past our imagination, and we think we have said enough in this small pamphlet, to convince our readers that Spiritualism is all humbug.

FINIS.

www.ingramcontent.com/pod-product-compliance
Lightning Source LLC
Chambersburg PA
CBHW082059070426
42452CB00052B/2753